From Parkinson's to a poet

Laughter and Tears Poetry Collection

M E L O D Y   E D D I N S

ARCHWAY
PUBLISHING

Scripture taken from the King James Version of the Bible.

Archway Publishing books may be ordered through booksellers or by contacting:

Archway Publishing
1663 Liberty Drive
Bloomington, IN 47403
www.archwaypublishing.com
1 (888) 242-5904

ISBN: 978-1-4808-3903-8 (sc)
ISBN: 978-1-4808-3904-5 (e)

Library of Congress Control Number: 2016918031

Print information available on the last page.

Archway Publishing rev. date: 12/19/2016

Contents

Special People and Places

Faith

When I Became a Christian

As I sat and listened to the preacher, he spoke of heaven and hell,
How we should want to go to heaven and forever there to dwell.
In hell, we will burn forever, but never are consumed,
For this is what we've chosen. Through life we are foredoomed.

He spoke of all the bad things throughout my life I've trod.
How could he know all these things? I thought he might be God!
I felt my heart in my throat, and my hands were wet with sweat
As I held on to the back of the pew, I knew I had to pay this debt.

Then he spoke of a man who died, forever to set us free.
His name is Jesus, and He loves whomsoever, and that means even me.
He bore the shame and punishment. Upon Him was the cross.
He carried it to Calvary, and there He died! Oh, what a loss!

I said, "Father, if You'll walk with me to the altar,
I will walk with You each day I live and try not to falter."
I took this preacher by the hand and said, "I need to be saved!"
He knelt down beside me and shared God's Word so brave.

I now call myself a Christian for my heart I gave to Christ,
I now must live my life to show His great sacrifice.
Don't worry about the outside and how you look to Him.
Just bring Him to the inside, and the outside He will trim.

God Speaks

Listen. What do you hear as you kneel and bow to pray?
Your heart beats fast when the Holy Spirit says, "Jesus is the way."
God speaks in so many ways; we have to listen just the same.
Try the spirits, bad or good. God speaks from where He came.

I've been through storms, and I thought, *How could this be?*
However, when God speaks, He says, "Come unto me."
When I am burdened and heavy-laden,
God says, "Come and rest, My dear children."

When the doctor says there is no hope,
Where do we turn, and how do we cope?
Jesus says, "I am the Great Physician!"
Our lives are His, and healing has begun.

When death comes knocking at our door,
We seem to think of time, and we want more—
To live, to laugh, to give to those we love,
And be a witness; awards we want from above.

For some are ready to stand alone
Before God, for life and sin to atone,
But for the rest, it will be too late
For God will banish, and in hell they will hate.

So let's be ready and prepared to go
When here on earth we hear the trumpet blow.
The graves will open, and the dead in Christ will rise,
And those who remain will meet them in the skies.

Forever and ever we'll live with Him,
The One who died for victory to win.
Jesus is the light; no need for the sun.
God says, "Well done, My Son and only one."

God's Angels

I've heard that angels have wings, but others say not.
Let's listen to what God says and see just what they've got.
God says they're heavenly creatures, created to give Him praise.
The angels sing with gladness when a sinner has been saved.

The angels can bring us a message and begin with, "Do not fear."
Behold, God wants you to know that He is ever so near.
For us down here upon the earth, the angels protect and serve.
They keep us from harm and bless us with
things that we don't even deserve.

So if you're in a place that's brought you to your knees,
Just bow your head, and ask God to send you an angel, please.
He'll send one down to intervene and sometimes take the blame,
Even when it's me, O Lord, who's caused all of this shame.

You can almost hear the angels as they shout with heaven's joy
When one more saint comes home for eternity to enjoy!
As I walk each day through life I look for angels unaware
For my journey into heaven I am living to prepare.

Creation

It's dark and void. There is no light.
Darkness then was called the night.
No waters or land could be seen—
Just nothing but black for there was no green.

All of a sudden a great voice spoke,
"Let there be light," and the darkness broke!
The firmament divided the water and land.
Heaven and earth are what God had planned.

He brought forth the herbs and grass
And all the fruit trees in His path.
He made the seasons and days of the year.
As He spoke, these things would appear.

He made every creature great and small,
From fish to elephants big and tall.
Be fruitful and multiply. Fill the land and sea.
Everything is good, you and I and Me.

In our image let us make man
To rule this land; we know he can.
It will take some help of Mine to give.
I send My Son to die that you might live.

Existence or Biblical Events

I heard an awesome sermon from a preacher tried and true.
He said if we're living, we're existing, not just passing through.
Sometimes there are events in life that will surely bring us down,
But if we follow Jesus, we can live life victorious and without a frown.

The story was told of a little boy who stuck his tongue to the freezer ice
After Mama had asked him to do a chore and was being ever so nice.
When he chose to disobey Mama, the lesson he learned that day
Was always do what Mama says, or on the ice your tongue may stay!

You see, Peter went fishing with friends and stayed awake all night,
But to their dismay, tired and weary, there was neither nibble nor bite.
Now when Jesus showed up at the boat, and Peter sat and listened,
Jesus said, "Go to the other side and fish,"
and Jesus even went with him.

Now this was an event in Peter's life and a lesson learned so well.
We could choose to live our lives our way or choose Him over hell.
I'll take my chances with the Lord for He's never let me down.
I know a friend or two who when times got rough could not be found.

I learned a lesson well that day; I remember all too well.
There have been events in my life only to God could I tell.
It's not good when we disobey. You don't have to tell me twice.
Always do what's right, or we might find our
tongues stuck to the freezer ice.

We can live our lives by the sins we commit, therefore guilty for life.
But Jesus gave His life on the cross so that
we could be free from all strife.
Don't let the events of this life determine how we'll live for Him
For I'd rather have Jesus and heaven for eternity to win!

I Was There

The Holy Spirit spoke to my heart and told me all things true.
He was the three in one, along with the Father and the Son, too.
He brought me to the foot of the cross to a sight of great despair,
And before my eyes it was Jesus; I was truly there!

He took my place; it should have been me upon the cross to die.
He looked ahead in time and said, "Child, don't you cry!
It's love that put Me on this cross, and it's love that makes Me stay,
For I could call the angels, and for Me they would make a way."

Through my walk He walks with me. In my trials He's been my stay.
When I kneel and pray, I'm always reminded
He's been there all the way.
There'll come a day—I know not when or where—
He'll show me all things tried and true. It's
heaven! My victory! I know I'm there!

I was there when they nailed Him to the tree and
was there when they laid Him in the tomb.
In the pits of hell He fought and won, and the
keys He brought to heaven and doom!
And when He rose on that third day, He rose in victory!
I was there. It wasn't just a dream! He's *alive* for you and me!

Mr. Henry and God

As a small boy I sat on the woodpile,
Listening to old Mr. Henry tell stories with a smile.
He would tell us about seeing God in the wood as he whittled
And formed the piece of virgin wood by hand into a whistle.

Mr. Henry, like most of the older gents,
would gather at the country store.
Every morning they told stories, true or
not, but to the truth they swore.
When Mr. Henry would tell a story, you knew you didn't have to ask,
Because he had either seen God or heard
from Him; He didn't wear a mask.

Whether looking at the sun, hot and bright,
or the moon, crescent or half,
Mr. Henry saw God or heard from God every
day, and this would be his epitaph.
He wasn't shy about telling people when God came walking by
In the hustle and bustle of the day, under the stars of the evening sky.

As a young boy who did not know my purpose or God's plan,
Mr. Henry got old and feeble, could hardly
see, and I became a young man.
He asked me one day to take him to the store
for something he needed badly.
As we walked in, the gents politely asked,
"Henry, have you seen God lately?"

With my hand on my heart and looking
up to God, this is what he said:
"I haven't been able to see much of anything lately but God."
Well, Mr. Henry died, but his stories live
on in the hearts of those like me.
I'm just a preacher boy, sharing the story
of Jesus who died to set us free.

It has been many years since Mr. Henry went to heaven.
I am older, looking forward to walking those streets so golden.
This story will continue through the contents of this poem
And tell of what talking to God, in our hearts, will become.

Story told to Calvary Baptist Church, Jefferson, South Carolina
by Pastor Robert Griggs, the young boy and preacher.
3/27/2016

Where Has My Faith Gone?

From the time I was small, I've heard how Jesus loves me,
How the Bible tells me so, and how He can set me free.
My parents drug me to church for every
service; singing and revival, too.
I knew the language and how to act, and
when it was time, I chose life anew.

I learned my ABCs: admit, believe, and confess.
I even learned how to and how not to dress.
I learned how Jesus died to set me free.
He promised me heaven for eternity.

All through my growing years, I tried to
live what they expected me to be.
The pastor, deacons, teachers, and family were the examples before me.
I finally got old enough and stepped into the world,
And oh my, the things I saw this world has unfurled!

I began to think and try to rationalize religion;
Things I used to believe in, had just become fiction.
There were questions like the goodness of God flooding my mind,
And why He allows bad things to happen to those who are so kind.

If it weren't for the nonbelievers, the believers would have no purpose.
But listen close, my child, as the Word of God is precious.
The church is a body of believers who live to serve Him.
It's the purpose of the nonbeliever to choose God or life ever so grim.

Now Baal was a god but not to be worshipped
For he tricked and lied to make this world wicked.
I know you've been taught from the time you were little
Not to talk to strangers or listen to their fables.

I would rather go with the ones who love me and know my heart
Than to be with those who lie and try to tear us apart.
Grace is God, giving to us what we do not deserve.
And mercy is God withholding judgment we do deserve.

Atheists say there is no God because they choose not to believe.
But I say there is no atheist for God says that
they, too, will bow and then leave.
Heaven is just for those who have kept the
faith and have actually never seen
What mercy and grace on Calvary's cross
actually meant for you and me.

I love you more than words can say, and a lie I would never tell.
Listen, child, before it's too late for there are no friends in hell.
Your family, church, and loved ones, too,
will kneel before God's throne,
But while we're still here on earth, we're praying for our own.

We all have a different purpose in this adventure called life.
And we only have one chance to make all things right.
Let's use the gifts and talents that were given by our Savior,
And live a life of service that in us He might find favor.

07/27/2015

Family

The Real Me

My daddy is half Yankee and my mama a southern belle.
So what does that make me? I will never tell.
Although I'm short in stature, a koala you may see,
But when I become a lady, a panda I may be.

Up to the mountains and down to the
beach, or Christmas ever so near;
It is things like family, friends, and traditions that I hold so dear.
Biscuits and gravy are my favorite food; my daddy cooks so well.
Memaw's chocolate brownies I think too are swell.

I've been taught to walk in a godly way and hold my head up high.
God made me perfect in every way, so to do my best, I will try.
Childhood memories flood my mind, but the best is yet to come.
As I spend my life with those I love, that's
where happiness comes from.

MAKENZIE EDDINS 1/11/16
WITH THE HELP AND GUIDANCE OF HER MEMAW, MELODY EDDINS.

13

Big Brother

In my childhood years, having a brother could be dangerous.
They would toot on your head and walk away, looking clueless.
They would push you off the side of the pool, knowing you can't swim,
But I would relish in the moment when Mama disciplined him.

They would try to get you to eat dirt, or even a worm or two,
And talk you into holding your breath until your face turned blue.
Who created brothers? It couldn't have been God
For brothers need to be disciplined completely by the rod.

As I think of all the bad things, there's some good to think of, too.
My brothers are all so cute, with their humor in full view.
They even let me play with them when a team they had to fill.
Even though I couldn't reach the goal, to me was such a thrill!

I remember there was a time, skating on the ice,
Playing tag and I was it, ahead to pay the price.
I slid down and cracked my chin but up again to play,
My big brother picked me up; no more playing today.

I looked down and saw the blood, my coat all soaked in red.
With frightful tears, he held me tight for he knew what was ahead.
Dr. Sen said that day, "Six stiches she will need,"
But all I needed that one day was my brother, I would plead.

Time has slipped by, and we're old almost as dirt.
One brother still I have; we share our grief and hurt.
He calls me all the time as I call on him as well,
Just to check and make sure we both are doing swell.

In memory of my brothers Harold and Harry Jr. Also in honor of my
brother Jerry2/21/2016

My Hero

Most people say a hero is someone with strength and courage,
like saving a life or giving their life. For you I have this message.
Let me tell you about my hero for he is a hero to me.
He fought in war and battle, too, so we in America can be free.

He's a quiet man of very few words, but if you listen when he speaks,
You know he's lived and learned a life that we all too should seek.
He's worked till he's tired and worn; his hands are calloused rough.
His steps are slower, but life goes on; in God he must trust.

He taught his children to speak the truth and never break a promise
for our word is what we stand on, our life to be so cautious.
We don't steal from others, and we protect what is our own.
We have that right through life for this is what we've known.

He doesn't show much emotion or talk of words of love,
But each day he puts love into action, and that is love from above.
He has a strong opinion of how people should work and live,
But most of what he thinks goes along with God, who forgives.

His family is his heart and life; his grands he spoils and pampers.
He teaches them how to bait a hook and drive a Farmall tractor.
I know we're coming to the end of a journey; over forty years we two.
But when death finally comes, I know I want
to stroll over heaven with you.

To my beloved husband
6/14/2015

Daddy of My Heart

From the first time he saw me and took my little hand,
Love grew between the two of us, a life so unplanned.
Even though I wasn't his, a daddy he became,
And no one could question for I was his to claim.

He used to pick with Mama and look at her and say,
"I fell in love with her, but with you I'll always stay."
The three of us were happy and a family from the start,
Maybe not from birth but always from the heart.

We had a little boy, and our family was complete.
Our lives were not always easy but always just as sweet.
Daddy never talked much, as Mama took the lead,
But Daddy was the head of the home, on this we all agreed!

Daddy's hands were always calloused from working hard each day.
When Daddy said our supper blessing, our hands folded as he prayed.
Each night when at bedtime we would run and get our love,
Daddy's hands were oh, so gentle, just like Jesus from above.

Daddy walked me down the aisle with my hand in his that day,
So gentle as he kissed me and to my husband he gave away.
It's been a lot of years now, with children of my own,
But there's nothing like seeing Daddy every time I go home.

I'm reminded of those gentle hands when with my children he plays
And always lets them win at checkers, and his chair he gives away.
Even though not from birth, I love my Daddy of my heart.
You see, it's love that makes a family from the start.

7/6/2015
IN HONOR OF JIM EDDINS AND DAUGHTER TANYA EDDINS JOHNSON.

Father and Son

A father walks impatiently, waiting for the birth.
A son is born, and oh, what joy fills the earth.
Smiles and giggles, tussles and wiggles, father and son to be.
The two in one, father and son, these are a pod of two peas.

Growing so fast, before long, you'll walk in Daddy's shoes.
It seems there is a shadow when Daddy makes a move.
He wants to be just like Daddy, with a hammer in his hand,
and always follow Jesus and for country take a stand.

Wherever you see one, you'll see the other too,
they work together every day, two peas in a pod, me and you.
They think alike and walk the same; on each other they depend.
And home they go, tired and weary, departing another day's end.

Playing ball and fishing, and watching NASCAR, too,
seems to be the favorite sport from the recliners they do view.
Family is important; love and loyalty they believe
that no matter what may come their way, faith and hope to achieve.

It seems that through the growing years, it's been just father and son.
The table has turned, and Father has learned
that now the son has won.
Although the shadow still lingers, it differs in its make,
Daddy now follows son with each step that he takes.

Oh, the memories that they made forever and a day
will always be in the hearts and minds for grands to make their way.
So as the clock strikes midnight, and all is quiet and still,
father and son are kneeling, asking God to show His will.

They pray for grace and mercy, and protection for their own,
and know that God is listening and watching from His throne.
Their faith never waivers in the storms that come at night.
Someday when they're in heaven, Father and Son will be their Light.

5/11/2015
IN HONOR OF MY HUSBAND AND SON,
JIMMY EDDINS SR. AND JIMMY EDDINS JR.

Sister Jude

She was twelve years older than me and bossy from the start.
She would scold me for the wrongs I did, but such a tender heart.
When she married her love and moved away from home,
I cried myself to sleep that night for I felt so alone.

When Mama went to heaven to live with Jesus there,
Jude came home and loved me, and our grief together we shared.
She became the figure of a mama that I no longer had.
Fit the part right nicely; she started her own family, I might add.

As the years quickly passed, and I, too, am now grown.
I married my love also and have children of my own.
Jude became a Christian, and to me she would tell
Of Jesus who had saved her from that awful place called hell.

She gave me my first Bible and wrote upon the page,
"II Timothy 2:15, study and need not be ashamed."
She also became my prayer warrior as she prayed for me each day.
The Holy Spirit spoke to me, and for me He made the way.

We would talk for hours on the phone for we lived so far apart.
We would share about our families and praise Jesus from our hearts.
Jude would talk about her children and her grands she loved so much.
She was such a mentor in the Lord; my life and heart she touched.

She could play the piano like no one else I've ever heard.
We would sing and sing and sing until the angels I thought we'd stirred.
Her fingers on the keys and her feet upon the pedals, a God-given miracle.
In her name, her church dedicated their new hymnals.

My sister now lives in heaven, and at times I feel alone,
But I know that she's with Jesus and kneeling at His throne.
Her grandson whom she raised from birth and loved oh so well,
Took her life so cruelly; life in prison he must dwell.

We still celebrate her birthday as if the candles she would blow.
I miss her smile, her pigeon toes, and even her bossy glow!
I still celebrate her life for she lived it with her heart
That she gave to Jesus long ago and promised never to depart.

7/6/2015
IN MEMORY OF MY SISTER JUDY FOOS DECKER.

Sisters

As the youngest of ten children, I often heard it said
That I was the spoiled one and always first in bed.
They said I always got my way by crying and whining, too.
But I lo seem to remember, my dear sister, it was you!

I always had to wear the hand-me-downs from sisters five
And hope that somehow, someway, I could just survive.
It wasn't very easy, being the youngest of them all.
I felt like Cinderella, never going to the ball.

My bark was bigger than my bite when at school I used to pick a fight,
Then run and hide behind you, a scaredy-cat with awful fright!
I remember to this day the words that you would say,
"In order to get to her, you have to move me out of the way!"

As the years crept slowly by, on each other to depend,
With Mom and Dad no longer here, you were my best friend.
It seemed each time that I would stumble and cause myself to fall,
You were there to pick me up; this, too, I do recall.

Although those times are over, on you I still depend
For you are my prayer warrior and always my best friend.
My sister, I do love you more than words could ever tell.
A picture speaks a thousand words, forever sisters, all is well.

5/19/2015
With my sister Pamela G. Woodiwiss.

Grand Ma

As my mind goes back to a younger year, about forty years or so,
This lady I did meet, her son had become my beau.
As I looked at her, and she looked at me,
I knew right then that one and one does make three.

After all the wedded bliss, our family began to grow,
First two, then three, then along came four with little Bo.
This lady that I met, with love and pride stood in awe,
When at first she heard our children call her Grandma!

Grandma, as I also affectionately would call her,
Since my own mother I barely knew
When God took her home to heaven.
This little girl thought, *How could this be true?*

Well, Grandma taught me many things that a mother would teach her own,
Like cooking and cleaning, canning and freezing, and never fearing the unknown.
Just take on life, live your best, and take care of those you love,
That someday when you're "ninety-six" you now we take care of.

She's lived her life to the fullest and talks to all who will listen.
She can't really see who she's talking to as she doesn't have much vision.
A disease has taken her eyesight, but her other senses work doubly hard,
Especially when she hears a child cry or a car pulling up in the yard.

She loves her children, and I am just as the girls, she'd say with a twinkle
in her eye,
I am her favorite daughter-in-law she'd be quick to reply.
You raise your kids and teach them well about God and His great plan,
To follow His path that He's laid for you, and never break His commands.

Time has passed, ninety-seven years this year, and her health has quickly failed.
Please, God, ease her pain, and prepare her journey; this is what we prayed.
We hoped she would be with us for her birthday ninety-seven,
but one day short, for this year she's with Jesus in heaven.

The family here we gather to celebrate our mother
and cherish each and every memory and share with one another.
Through all these years never a cross word; I still stand in awe
of the lady I met forty years ago, will always be Grand Ma!

APRIL 21, 2015
YOUR FAVORITE DAUGHTER-IN-LAW.

One Kind Soul

Oh, how precious it is to look into the face of your first granddaughter!
So, at peace as you lay on mommy's chest amid your slumber.
You were such a fiesty little thing, and the
faces you made were priceless!
Born between two brothers, sometimes being
a tomboy, yet, always a little princess.

You would sit in Papaw's chair with a book and listen to him read,
As soon as he said *"The End"*, you took the
book, let me read you would plead.
Memaw's job was to spoil you, to watch over
you when you were not aware.
I prayed for God's protection, and taught you
right, for this world we need beware.

Growing up was not always easy, many obstacles in the way,
But knowing God was in control, in His will you would stay.
I watched you as you grew, like a hummingbird with wings.
You became our little "song bird", the nightingale as she sings.

As time quickly passes, you became a young lady before our eyes.
Wisdom usually comes with age, but you my dear, the one so wise.
I know you love God, and your family too,
But there is another love someday you will find to be true.

Always stay the way you are now, a kind soul down deep.
Looking for ways to serve God, opportunity you must leap.
Always be faithful to God, and all hopes and dreams will come to be,
But always be mindful to trust and obey and pray on bended knee.

I love you dear and proud as proud can be,
To be your memaw, and know that you love me!
Remember I am always watching and praying for your protection,
For there are times we all stand in need of God's correction.

Go ahead and spread your wings, and fly to places unknown;
For I will always be here when you want to come back home.
Love God first, and your family too, and serve within your church.
Lay up your treasures in Heaven, for on Earth there is no worth.

In honor of my first granddaughter, Savannah Johnson
11/11/2015

Mama's Hands

When I was little you would take my hand,
As we walked to church, I would kick the sand.
We worked in the fields from dawn to dusk,
And in the winter barn, the corn we would husk.

Even when grown, in the summer we would gather,
Our hands working in vegetables, our tongues to chatter.
You loved your flowers and could name them one by one.
The blooms would multiply, for they were your passion.

The years went by and God blessed you with grands...
You loved them all and would help them stand.
You would take their hand and lead them to to walk,
while laughing at the funny little words,, as they began to talk.

You used your hands to cook, and to help those in need.
At night, you would lay with a flashlight, just so you could read.
As your eyes became dim, and could read no more,
You felt in your spirit the decisions of war.

You lived your last years with a daughter so dear,
But the others were there when you needed them near.
You held our hand from the time we were born.
We now hold your hand in death, together we mourn.

We know you are in Heaven, as Jesus took your hand,
Walking on gold streets in that heavenly land.
You are waiting for your family from Heaven above,
Reaching out to us, to welcome, with your hand of love.

CHRISTMAS 2015

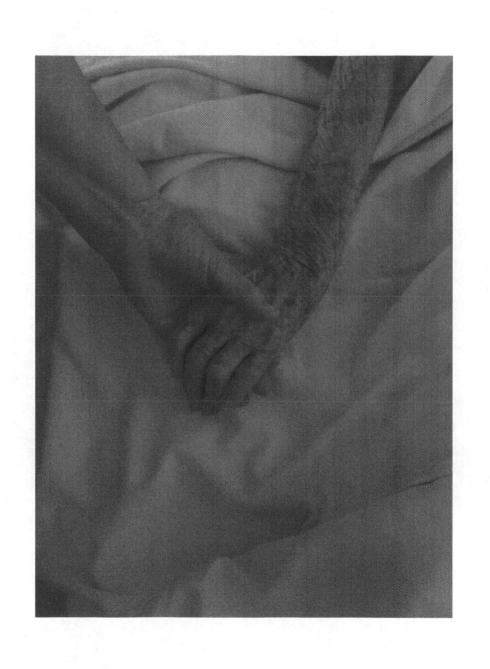

Reflections through the Eyes of the Appalachians

Over a thousand miles do these trails extend.
From Maine to Georgia, with nature, befriend.
Hundreds of trails are traveled by hikers each year,
With a dream and a passion, and the whisper they often hear.

No sleep tonight, so up before dawn with gear on our backs,
We start on our journey—hey, this is easy—we're making tracks!
One foot and then the other; it didn't take long for reality to hit.
Return from whence I came, I started to quit.

As we journeyed through the trails, our view beyond words,
Colors so vibrant, animals talking, and the singing of the birds.
As we reached the campsite, we settled in for the night.
There were blisters on my feet, and my muscles, oh so tight!

I asked myself this question, "Why do I put myself through this?"
Then the Holy Spirit reminds me only through Jesus am I His.
I know that without Him, I couldn't do this on my own.
I am absolutely nothing till I reach His heavenly throne.

The remoteness and solitude give me time to think
So deeply about my life; it could end in just a blink.
I have a better appreciation for those whom I love so dear.
I bow my head in prayer and say, "God, keep us ever so near."

These mountains are meant to be traveled
by those who are far and near.
Listen for God to speak, for in whom shall you fear?
I know I have to keep going until I reach the end
For these mountains will always keep calling, whispering in the wind.

IN HONOR OF MY SON-IN-LAW, KEVIN JOHNSON
02/20/2016

Silence

I feel the beat of my heart and the gentle breeze as it blows.
I can see the running stream but no sound as the water flows.
I cannot hear my heartbeat or the wind as it gently whistles.
I can see the happy faces of the children full of giggles.

I feel my mother's footsteps as she walks into my room.
I feel the wet tears my mother cried; I wonder, *For whom?*
She thinks I am asleep as she bends and kisses my cheek.
Then I realize her burden is for me as I quickly take a peek.

You see, I have been deaf since a baby in the womb.
Sometimes when people look at me, I wonder what they assume.
I was born without ears, and my eardrums still need to form.
But I know how smart I am and how people are misinformed.

I have hopes and dreams like any little boy should have,
Like hiding from Mama and playing ball with Dad.
A doctor, astronaut, or just like my daddy, tailor-made.
I know God made me perfect for in His image I was made.

I have these little ear muffs Mommy and Daddy make me wear.
They make me look like a video junkie, but I don't give a care.
I can hear my heartbeat and the wind as it gently whistles.
My Mommy's not sad, and I can hear the children giggle!

I will hear the beat of the music and dance to the melody until dawn.
She's my love, my everything, our lives to build upon.
As we dance around the room, arm in arm to adore,
I will hear the "I love you"; we're together forevermore.

You see, I have a handicap, but I can do things on my own.
I pray for strength and courage for I know I'm not alone.
Someday when I become a dad, I will hear their little cries,
But love is from the heart; no need to ask the whys.

In honor of my precious great-nephew, Owen Griggs.
Mama and Daddy are Shawn and Jenny Griggs of
Jenera, Ohio; along with older sister Olivia, and brothers, Brady and
Jared.

6/25/2015

Creation / Nature

Butterflies

You know, I wasn't always as pretty as I am today.
It takes a lot of time, and I sometimes get dismayed.
I began as an egg placed on a plant of host,
Then emerge as a caterpillar, smaller than most.

I eat to remain strong for metamorphous to complete.
I'll go through many stages, which often to repeat.
I finally come to the place wrapped up so snug and tight,
Waiting for the day, the sun I'll see so bright!

I'm going through a change while waiting for the day
I become a beautiful butterfly, able to fly away.
It only takes a few days for that special time,
Breaking loose from my bed to a world so sublime.

My wings span out with beauty of design
As someone watches me, a feeling so divine.
I was created for a purpose all my own,
To reproduce this beauty, the world has never known.

The next time you see a butterfly, oh so pretty,
Think of me and this poem written with much envy.
There may not be butterflies in heaven;
Enjoy us here on earth for by the Father you are given.

02/28/2016

Walking in the Rain

Walking in the rain on a spring afternoon.
No thunder or lightning; just a shower before the moon.
My mind wanders back to a place so dear.
A child was I; my life so clear.

Happy I was, running in the rain,
With my goulashes on and cold in my veins.
The puddle was there, not me, but who?
Oh no! The puddle just swallowed my shoe!

When the rain was over and the mud it left,
It was time for cooking and baking just like mother.
I remember her well, although she's gone now.
She would always bake a cake to be kind to another.

As my mind races back to the here and now,
I see a big puddle; it's reflecting back to me.
It's daring me to do what I haven't done in years.
I jumped on in, and it went up to my knee!

It felt so good to just be a kid again,
Remembering the good, the bad to let go.
As I look to my right and look to my left,
So beautiful and bright, the colors of a rainbow.

02/01/2016

The Appalachian Trail

As a child, a little on the chubby side, I would sit with head in hand
And wonder what it would be like to hike across this land.
I wasn't very sporty, always sitting on the side to watch,
But when it came to technology, I was always topnotch!

I learned to play the piano, and school was just a breeze.
Now married with children, working, and
college, no time to even breathe!
As I settled into the corporate world, and family to and fro,
I did all things I thought I should to help my family grow.

Some say it's just a midlife crisis, but I know I hear the call
Of the Appalachian Trail with its trees and mountains so tall!
So I gathered up some gear and my sons who were so young.
It didn't take me long; I stopped and my hammock I had hung.

When hiking you feel the gentle breeze, and the air is oh, so clean.
You hear the rushing flow of the clear and crystal stream.
You know it didn't just evolve from a tiny little dot
For the beauty of this land was created without spot.

We've hiked through many trails, and miles behind us now,
But many miles in front of us to complete for I have made this vow.
When I get past this midlife crisis, for grands I'll tell this tale,
How this chubby little boy climbed the Appalachian Trail.

02/18/2016

Special People and Places

Butterflies

You know, I wasn't always as pretty as I am today.
It takes a lot of time, and I sometimes get dismayed.
I began as an egg placed on a plant of host,
Then emerge as a caterpillar, smaller than most.

I eat to remain strong for metamorphous to complete.
I'll go through many stages, which often to repeat.
I finally come to the place wrapped up so snug and tight,
Waiting for the day, the sun I'll see so bright!

I'm going through a change while waiting for the day
I become a beautiful butterfly, able to fly away.
It only takes a few days for that special time,
Breaking loose from my bed to a world so sublime.

My wings span out with beauty of design
As someone watches me, a feeling so divine.
I was created for a purpose all my own,
To reproduce this beauty, the world has never known.

The next time you see a butterfly, oh so pretty,
Think of me and this poem written with much envy.
There may not be butterflies in heaven;
Enjoy us here on earth for by the Father you are given.

02/28/2016

Walking in the Rain

Walking in the rain on a spring afternoon.
No thunder or lightning; just a shower before the moon.
My mind wanders back to a place so dear.
A child was I; my life so clear.

Happy I was, running in the rain,
With my goulashes on and cold in my veins.
The puddle was there, not me, but who?
Oh no! The puddle just swallowed my shoe!

When the rain was over and the mud it left,
It was time for cooking and baking just like mother.
I remember her well, although she's gone now.
She would always bake a cake to be kind to another.

As my mind races back to the here and now,
I see a big puddle; it's reflecting back to me.
It's daring me to do what I haven't done in years.
I jumped on in, and it went up to my knee!

It felt so good to just be a kid again,
Remembering the good, the bad to let go.
As I look to my right and look to my left,
So beautiful and bright, the colors of a rainbow.

02/01/2016

The Appalachian Trail

As a child, a little on the chubby side, I would sit with head in hand
And wonder what it would be like to hike across this land.
I wasn't very sporty, always sitting on the side to watch,
But when it came to technology, I was always topnotch!

I learned to play the piano, and school was just a breeze.
Now married with children, working, and
college, no time to even breathe!
As I settled into the corporate world, and family to and fro,
I did all things I thought I should to help my family grow.

Some say it's just a midlife crisis, but I know I hear the call
Of the Appalachian Trail with its trees and mountains so tall!
So I gathered up some gear and my sons who were so young.
It didn't take me long; I stopped and my hammock I had hung.

When hiking you feel the gentle breeze, and the air is oh, so clean.
You hear the rushing flow of the clear and crystal stream.
You know it didn't just evolve from a tiny little dot
For the beauty of this land was created without spot.

We've hiked through many trails, and miles behind us now,
But many miles in front of us to complete for I have made this vow.
When I get past this midlife crisis, for grands I'll tell this tale,
How this chubby little boy climbed the Appalachian Trail.

02/18/2016

Special People and Places

Little Jeremy

Jeremy was not quite like the other children, but each day he went to school.
He didn't learn as fast as some; at times, the kids were cruel.
He tried so hard but came up short; the tests were oh, so hard!
The teacher worked with him, never showing disregard.

Jeremy's parents were called to the school to hear the awful news.
Jeremy couldn't come to school anymore; another they must choose.
They said it wasn't fair to the other kids, their time was just as vital.
But Jeremy knew each child's name, and the teacher was his idol.

The teacher knew within her heart that Jeremy could learn with time;
Someone with knowledge and patience could help him as he climbed.
You see, even though he was small in stature, twelve years old was he.
Still in the second grade, it didn't bother him, but it would bother you and me.

It was almost time for Easter break, and the class she could not silence,
So nineteen eggs she handed out and offered them her guidance.
She wanted them to fill the egg of something that represents new life.
She became excited for the following day, for nineteen eggs were dyed.

She knew one had to belong to Jeremy; when she found it, joy just trilled her heart,
But when she saw it was empty inside, she wanted to hide it from the start.
But Jeremy, calling, "Teacher, Teacher," he was excited as could be.
He shouted, "They killed Jesus, laid Him in the grave, but He rose in victory
for you and me!"

You see, the empty egg represented the empty tomb where Jesus had laid that day.
So even though the egg was empty, it was still full of life for Jesus is the way.
Jeremy may not know how to read and write, like most his age could do,
But he knew in his heart that Jesus is life, the egg and the empty tomb.

WRITTEN FROM A STORY TOLD AT CALVARY BAPTIST CHURCH BY
PASTOR ROBERT GRIGGS
04/15/2001S

Going into the Hospital

Now I lay me down to sleep,
I pray the Lord my soul to keep.
When I wake up just before dawn,
when I get there, privacy will be gone.

They'll give me something to make me smile,
But when I wake up, no smile for a while!
Pain and stiffness; will there be no end?
Drugs, PT, and TLC will all be my friends.

They put these funny gowns that fasten in the back,
But as I walk the hall, all will see my backpack!
The doctors and nurses are working hard
To make sure when I go home I have a safeguard.

They'll poke and prod till dignity is no more,
And they'll know me better than they did before!
I'll be good with my, "Yes, ma'am," and, "No, sir,"
But holler a word or two if they make me any worse!

My family is always here for me just when I need them the most.
God never leaves me, always listens to me, for He is the upmost.
I don't have a worry, not a sorrow, nor a care
For Jesus is my Savior; I bow my head in prayer.

Having surgery, indeed, is not a fun thing to do
But sometimes necessary to make some parts new.
Thanks for the prayers and the love shown each day.
Each day will bring strength, and faith will be my stay.

08/11/2015

46

Happy Father's Day

As we celebrate Father's Day, let's look at what a father should be.
Not everyone has that honor; for some, a father, it's not he.
He's not a baby's daddy that just supplied a need.
He's a man on whom a child can depend, for this is what they plea.

From the time a child is born, Daddy is always there
with hugs and smiles, and always time to share.
He teaches them to ride their bikes and bait a fishing hook
or sit down for a little tea time or even read a book.

Each morning he wakes to hear the giggles and joins in all the fun,
then off to work for a full day's pay until a full day's pay is done.
He's met at the door with welcomed smiles from tiny faces aglow.
They want Daddy's time for today's activities to show.

Whether he teaches them about music or how to hit a nail,
He tells them to always do their best and for that they'll never fail.
He teaches them about life, disappointments will come their way,
but always turn the negative too positive;
there will always come a new day.

He teaches them right from wrong, and consequences to face
for each decision made hastily, confusion to replace.
But when they learn to follow the Lord in everything they do,
they follow that example that only Daddy can lead them through.

Happy Father's Day, 2015
06/16/2015

Huggy Mama

Mama exercises at the gym, so daddy's eyes will see her only.
She takes me to the day care, where I am oh so lonely.
Mama likes to cuddle close and hugs me all the time,
But dropping off a kid like this should really be a crime.

I'm smarter than she thinks I am, so I will throw a fit.
She'll pick me up and cuddle close, and to my cries submit.
So down the hall we go; in my stroller I think real quick,
"Huggy Mama! Huggy Mama!" But she knows it's just a trick.

She says, "We'll huggy when the stroller
stops," but I know what that means.
She's gonna leave me anyway to work out on those machines.
I keep saying, "Huggy Mama," but she just smiles to say,
"Mama will come and get you when I'm done and off to weigh."

I wish I had another mama, one who wouldn't leave me like this.
I look around the room, and I see something quite amiss.
There are other babies in here, and no tears in their eyes.
Their faith is in their mamas; they will never hear good-byes.

Jesus, please forgive me for my mama I do love.
She feeds me, cleans me; Mama's love is always from above.
An hour has passed, and I look out in the hall.
I see my mama all sweaty, for me she'd come to call.

She smiles at me, and I smile at her.
She says, "Huggy baby"; from there it was just a blur.
She puts me in the car, and off to home we go.
My eyes slowly close to sleep; I feel Mama's love I know.

02/21/2016

The Battle Flag

It seems there is a controversy about this flag and why it flies.
To some a symbol of history and the sound of battle cries.
To others, they see hate and the slaves of all the masters.
The beatings, the hangings, the nightly raids of the maskers.

Some want to give it respect for what it stood for way back when,
but others want it down for the memory it's always been.
When it still flew freely on the southern statehouse grounds.
If you listened very carefully, you could hear the battle sounds.

The battles are still raging, not between the North and South,
but by people with twisted minds and rantings from their mouths.
They use their guns and ammo to kill the innocent blood,
and some may even use politics to get their evil done.

Whether it flies or comes down, I have nothing to say;
I didn't live way back then, so neither a yes nor a nay.
So just remember this as you back and forth debate,
through Jesus forgiveness comes when at His feet we pray.

We are one nation under God, no matter from where we began.
We become united in brotherhood, and for freedom we take a stand.
We need to teach our young people by example that Jesus led
For every time innocent blood is spilled, the color still runs red.

Life is short and time surely flies; we still got a lot to do.
Don't have time for fussing and fighting,
but time to make all things new.
Everyone come together, and clasp the hand next to me
As we bow our heads together from sea to shining sea.

IN MEMORY OF:
THE NINE WHO LOST THEIR LIVES WHILE ATTENDING A BIBLE STUDY AT
THE EMMANUEL AME CHURCH IN CHARLESTON, SC ON JUNE 18, 2015
06/23/2015

The Beat of a Mother's Heart

Just imagine hearing the beat of a mother's heart
When she hears her baby's heartbeat from the start.
She feels little man's moves from way down deep inside,
Each time smiling with such gratitude and pride.

Whether it's finding his toes or making that first turn,
Mama feels her heart skip a beat for baby to learn.
She knows in her heart there's no stopping her child,
One day this child will conquer the world as she smiled.

She walks the floor with worry at night.
The fever is high, so she rocks until daylight.
Just teething, the doctor happily confirms,
While mom's heart skips a beat but is steady and firm.

Whether it be giggles, parties, cheers, or shouts,
And ball games, and singing, here and there about.
Even though she is tired and worn from the day,
She'll get up in the morning, and do it the same way.

That special day has finally arrived.
Twelve years in school for this he has strived.
As they call his name loud and clear,
Mama, with pride, smiling from ear to ear.

Now we don't know what's behind that smile,
If it's this or that; it may take a while.
Not sure of her feelings for her heart is full.
Off to college, she can feel the pull.

Her mind begins to wander to a place she's been before—
The first time she heard that heartbeat, and hers began to soar!
She knew she brought him up right, on Jesus to depend.
Her heart is now at peace in poetry she has penned.

01/19/2016

This Thing Called Life

Where does this thing called life come from?
Where does it begin, and where does it end?
Some roads we travel are straight and narrow,
while others are wide at every bend.

When we come into this world
we have nothing to give.
We are truly dependent on others
to show us how to live.

Well, those who set the example for us
have an obligation to fulfill.
Be honest and fair, trustworthy with care,
and an inner faith to instill.

Stealing and lying, cheating and backbiting
will only lead us astray.
Life is what we make of it,
good or bad, one heartbeat away.

We make choices each and every day,
And what kind of attitude we'll show.
We can either be bitter or better;
Which one will make us grow?

From the moment we're born
We begin to die.
But at the moment of death,
We begin to live, no more to cry.

02/01/2016

Valentine's Day

Love is in the air, and Cupid roams to and fro,
God of love, son of Venus, with his arrows and his bow.
A small, winged boy, blindfolded, born from a silver egg,
Shoots the arrow straight into the heart; desire for love we beg.

We ask for candy that will last not long,
And flowers so beautiful, but won't stay strong.
A candlelit dinner just for two.
That means no kids, no in-laws, just me and you!

Now Cupid is a myth to wonder of truth,
For is he real or just dreams of our youth?
One tale spoke of his mother's mischievous life
That backfired when Cupid took Psyche as his wife.

I can tell you of a man who is tried and true.
His name is Jesus, and He died for me and you.
He said man is to love his wife as he loves the church,
And wives, only to our husbands for love we search.

If you're single and looking for that special one,
Just make sure they're approved by the Son.
Save yourself for that special wedding day.
When two become one, your marriage will stay.

02/12/2016

Walking with Parkinson's Disease

When did these symptoms first appear?
When did I notice anxiety and fear?
I could not smell the roses after a springtime shower.
Sleepless nights, awake, it seems like hour upon hour.

My arms and legs became tight and rigid,
Not to mention the tremors ever so vivid!
What is happening to the body that God blessed me with?
Maybe it's His fault, and He's just another myth!

It seems I can't remember; words would just be lost.
I think I'm losing my mind; I have to know—whatever the cost!
When the doctor spoke those words, I could not catch my breath
For I just received my destiny, a slow and painful death.

Well, with learning there comes knowledge, so now I'm not afraid
To walk this journey to the end; to God I now have prayed.
I told Him I was sorry for calling Him a myth,
And He said not to worry, for me He'll always be with.

As I walk this journey, I may stumble and fall.
I may even freeze at times or have no expression at all.
I continue to shake, rattle, and roll,
But there will always be peace way down in my soul.

I know there is a blessing for me each and every day
As family, friends, and support groups always make a way.
I will smile in the face of having PD, dare to take my soul.
I'm sorry to disappoint you, PD, but heaven is my goal.

So I will live each day as if it were my last.
Who knows, it might not be PD; maybe driving way too fast.
Whatever it is that takes me out,
I've enjoyed living life, now in heaven I can shout!

11/24/2015

What I Want My Valentine to Be

I don't have much imagination, but I'm clear on what I want.
I'm old, I'm tired, so no need to put up a front.
I have bulges where there shouldn't be, and rolls beyond compare.
But in a man, my valentine, listen close, beware!

My valentine stands six feet tall, and handsome as can be,
With hair, a tint of gray, and eyes looking just at me.
He opens doors and holds my hand when walking in the park.
He finds a bench, sits me down, and then begins to spark.

Well, back in the old days, sparkin' was just sweet talk.
Let's just skip that part and get on with the lip lock.
He gives me flowers and candy, too,
But I say, "All I want is you!"

He has his arms around me and doesn't seem to mind
The bulges, the rolls, and other atrocities he may find.
His lips meet mine, and in the blink of an
eye, I'm back where it began.
I only dream this once a year, and once a year he's my man.

As reality hits, he's five foot eight and round as he is tall.
He's never given flowers, and the candy, he eats it all.
He doesn't know the word "romance"; he just says, "Come in here!"
I shuffle and get into bed with my valentine of forty years.

02/02/2016

Love, that Special Feeling

"What does love feel like?" I ask myself today.
Sometimes I thought I knew by actions or display.
Love is not just words we say to family, friends, and such,
But using what we have to give to a life we might touch.

Parents love their children from the time they are conceived.
Children are a blessing that from God we have received.
It's holding that newborn baby for the very first time.
And children obey and respect their parents for this, too, shall rhyme.

Love between siblings is a bond like no other.
They fuss and fight but always take up for sister and brother.
When life is going from bad to worse, and nothing seems to fit,
We always listen to each other, offer advice, knowledge, and wit.

Now there is a special feeling in the air when he and she first meet.
It comes from way down deep inside, the two are now complete.
He opens the box as she cries with joy while he's on bended knee.
To love someone more than we love our selves, this would be my plea.

There is no greater love than that of God who died to set us free.
In hell He fought and won the battle for in His hand was the key.
He rose in victory on that third day, now with His Father He stands
And waits for His Father to turn and say, "Go
get My children!" He commands.

01/18/2016

Motherly Love

From the time a mother has conceived and hears
the heartbeat of her precious little one,
A love that is like no other begins and reaches
through time; for eternity it is never done.
She realizes that child was given to her by an Almighty God,
Who in turn, is willing to dedicate that child
back to God, to Him we do applaud!

Motherly love is not just words written on a paper.
It is feelings for a child greater than herself.
She's willing to do anything to protect from harm
and danger, and even from oneself.
To encourage her child to reach for dreams and helping in the process.
To see her children reach for greater heights
and to always do what's best.

She prays for them daily that they will follow
the leading of God in their lives.
She sets a godly example for them to follow, and as they grow, be wise.
Even though she vowed to never let go, the time
comes when her children leave her nest.
Her love is greater than the unknown paths, and
she prays for this is the ultimate test.

Those prayers are answered each day to know
that God has them in His hands
And will never leave them or let them go,
for truth and honor as they stand.
She feels the pride while spending time with her
grandchildren God gave from above.
She smiles within her heart that God is the one
who has blessed beyond a mother's love.

CHRISTMAS 2014

Straight Down the Middle

There is a question flooding my mind
Of the different opinions in this world I find.
I wish I knew how to explain the truth,
Not just nursery rhymes heard from youth.

There are moral issues such as gay rights,
And abortion stealing a baby's birthright.
Even the Confederate flag to fly or not to fly.
Who's telling the truth, and who's telling a lie?

We won't look in the Bible for scripture always true,
Not even the Supreme Court and all of its clues.
Let's all just look at things natural and see what fits,
Then you make your decision from all of these tidbits.

When we look at the anatomy of woman and man,
Some parts fit, and others try if they can.
It's like working in a machine shop with tool and die;
It's not gonna fit no matter how hard they try!

I have loved ones who are gay and happy as can be.
I just live my life before them, and before God give my plea.
Sometimes it's hard to stay quiet and still,
But wait for that special love in their hearts for God to fill.

When a woman has an abortion, a decision she has made.
Of course, it is her right, but who has she betrayed?
There are some awesome couples, looking for babies just to love.
And they would raise your child if for
reasons you couldn't take care of.

To fly or not to fly, divided down the middle.
Between the North and South, it's become just a riddle.
The Confederate flag flew proudly for a colony in war,
Just as our American flag flies proudly and what she stands for.

Now let's just get real and look at what is right.
Don't let your mind play tricks on you and confusion to incite.
What's right is right and wrong is wrong, no matter the outside look.
It's when we look inside the heart, it becomes an open book.

To speak the truth is to speak God's Word.
We have it to read and study, not just what we've heard.
We have to believe every word, jot, and tittle.
It's the Inspired Word of God for there is no middle.

06/30/15

Thank you to Michael J Fox Foundation and The National Parkinson's Foundation for their encouragement and support. Both foundations work endlessly to put this disease to extinct by researching, and experimenting with new and innovative drugs and therapies. Most of all, they are searching for a cure to this disabling disease.

After cost, the profits and proceeds of this book will be donated to the Michael J Fox foundation for research and a cure. Melody also donates to the National Parkinson's Foundation, and hopes that everyone who reads her book will donate for a cure as well.

Please visit these websites:

www.melodyeddins-poetry.com

https://www.michaeljfox.org

www.parkinson.org

ABOUT THE AUTHOR

Melody Eddins was diagnosed with Parkinson's disease in 2011, and she is now retired after working until 2014. She began writing as therapy, where putting words together and creating rhymes helped her speak the words with ease. Even with Parkinson's, Melody loves life and enjoys writing about faith, family, and her experiences. Melody currently lives in Jefferson, South Carolina.